Contents

1. The Little Colt's Task   2

2. Friends   8

3. Watch and Pray   14

4. The Payment for Our Sins   21

5. Placed in a Tomb   28

6. He Has Risen   34

7. Floating to Heaven   41

Blessings!
Kelly Pulley

1
The Little Colt's Task

As Jesus neared Jerusalem, he sent some friends ahead.
"Go into the village where a colt awaits," he said.

"Untie the colt and bring it here. If someone there should ask,
just say to them, 'It's for the Lord. He needs it for a task.'"

Now when the two arrived in town, they found the colt was there.
But as the friends untied its reins, the owners stopped the pair.

"Why have you untied our colt?" they sternly asked the two.
"It's for the Lord," the friends replied, as Jesus said to do.

Jerusalem

3

They took the colt to Jesus. Cloaks were spread upon its back.
He slowly rode the colt away. Its hooves tapped *click-a-clack!*

As Jesus neared Jerusalem, the people gathered 'round.
Then some removed the cloaks they wore and laid them on the ground.

Still others spread the leaves of palms along the rocky track.
The beast of burden ambled on to taps of *click-a-clack!*

The crowd grew large, the crowd grew loud.
They cheered as Jesus came.
They shouted, "Glory to the Lord!"
and praised his holy name.

He entered through the city gate
upon the donkey's back.
The people cheered too loud to hear
the taps of *click-a-clack*.

Jerusalem now rose above
the dusty city street.
The sound of tapping stopped,
and Jesus stood upon his feet.

The little colt had done its task
and walked the rocky track,
announcing Jesus had arrived
to taps of *click-a-clack!*

2

Friends

Jesus sat with his friends eating supper and talking.
Then taking a basket of bread,
he gave thanks for the bread, and he broke it to pieces.
"Take this, it's my body," he said.

Then he picked up his cup and gave thanks for the wine.
"Drink this, it's my blood shed for you
so that many can have the forgiveness of sins."
His friends wondered, *Is this really true?*

Then glancing around at their faces, he said,
"One of you will betray me, it's true."
They looked at each other and asked one another,
"But who? Is it me? Is it you?"

"It's he who dips bread in the same bowl as I."
Judas said to him, "Surely not I?"
"Yes, it's you," Jesus said. "Quickly do what you must."
Judas left him without a reply.

Then Jesus said, "Children, my time here is short.
I say to you, love one another.
I'm going to make a place ready for you.
In the meantime, show love to each other."

3

Watch and Pray

Jesus took his friends
to find a quiet place to pray.
The Mount of Olives seemed
the perfect place to get away.

"Please watch and pray," he told them
as he wandered off alone.
He found a place among the trees.
He knelt there on his own.

He said, "Oh, Father, if you would,
please take this cup away.
But let it be as you would wish.
It's not for me to say."

Returning to his faithful friends,
he found that they were dozing.
They'd tried their best to watch and pray,
but soon their eyes were closing.

He said, "You couldn't watch an hour?"
but as his words came out,
a mob with torches, swords, and clubs,
appeared all 'round about.

Then from the shadows, Judas stepped.
His kiss would be the cue,
the signal to the mob to start
the job they'd come to do.

The men advanced with clubs and swords,
the mob was drawing near.
When Peter drew his sword and swung,
he severed someone's ear.

Then Jesus said, "Enough of this!"
He healed the injured man.
"This thing is meant to happen
to fulfill my Father's plan."

4

The Payment for Our Sins

When Jesus stood before the priests, they asked him, "Tell us, do.
Are you the Christ, the Son of God?" He answered, "Yes, it's true."

They thought that he had lied to them, believing him a fake.
They took him to the governor. His life they meant to take.

Then Pilate questioned Jesus as the priests had asked him to.
"Are you the king of all the Jews?" And Jesus said, "It's true."

He hadn't broken any laws, and Pilate told them so.
But still the leaders and the priests said, "Jesus has to go!"

The leaders whipped the people up into an angry mob.
They filled the people's hearts with hate to finish off the job.

The people shouted, "Crucify!" They wanted Jesus dead.
Though Pilate meant to set him free, he gave him up instead.

24

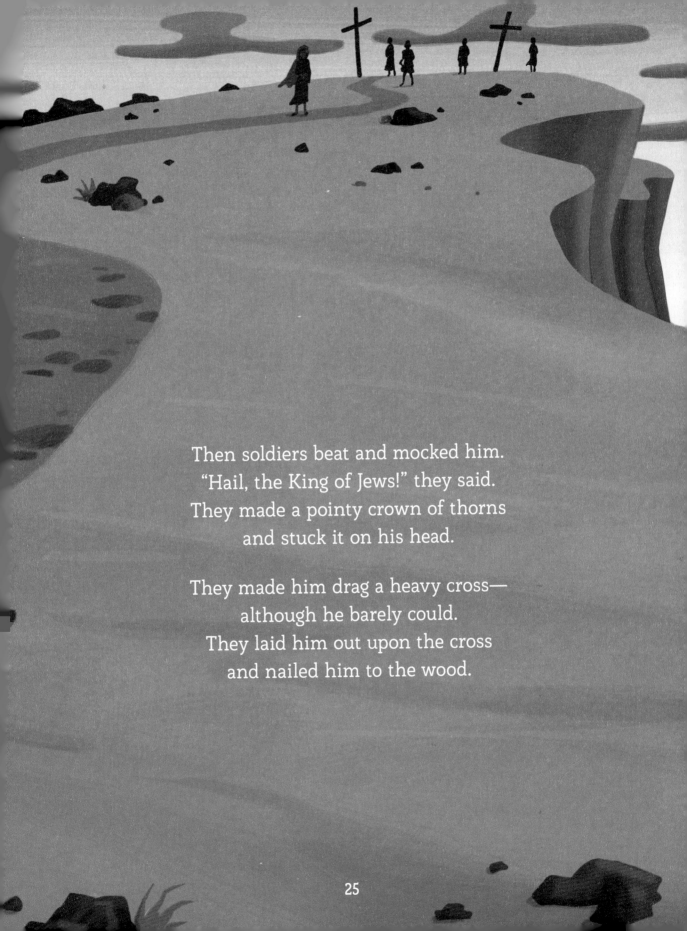

Then soldiers beat and mocked him.
"Hail, the King of Jews!" they said.
They made a pointy crown of thorns
and stuck it on his head.

They made him drag a heavy cross—
although he barely could.
They laid him out upon the cross
and nailed him to the wood.

They raised his cross. And there he died.
The sky turned black as night.
The ground began to shake and quake.
The guards cried out in fright.

The day he died was not the end.
Believe and life begins!
For Jesus died for everyone,
the payment for our sins.

5

Placed in a Tomb

After Jesus had died, he was placed in a tomb.
It was sealed with a stone to keep thieves from the room.

Roman soldiers stood guard at the tomb night and day
so that no one could carry his body away.

Then on day number three, in the morning's first light,
the guards at the tomb had a terrible fright.

The earth began shaking and quaking and rocking.
The guards began trembling, their knees began knocking.

They were shocked. They were spooked.
They were scared and alone.
But the worst thing of all—
over there by the stone—

An angel appeared!
He was dressed all in white!
His clothes were as bright
as a lightning bolt's light!

He pushed on the stone,
and he rolled it aside.
They were too scared to speak.
They were too scared to hide!

They were too scared to run. They decided instead . . .
to just lie on the ground and pretend they were dead!

So they did. Then the angel just sat on the stone.
He sat, and he waited and left them alone.

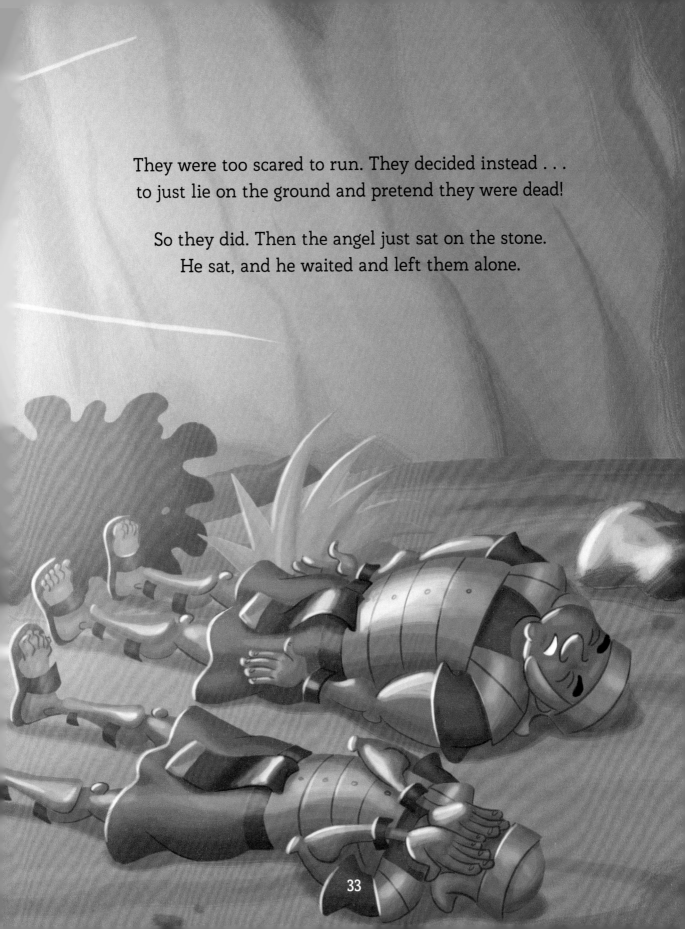

6

He Has Risen!

Three women arrived at the site of the tomb.
They were Jesus' friends, who brought spice and perfume.

But the stone had been moved, and now Jesus was gone.
They could see in the tomb by the light of the dawn.

Then an angel appeared. He said, "Don't be afraid.
Jesus is not in the place he was laid.

"He has risen! So go! And explain to his friends that his story goes on. This is not where it ends."

When the women arrived where the others had hid,
they described what they'd seen, they described what they did.

But the friends thought it nonsense. They didn't believe.
How could Jesus have simply decided to leave?

Well, they thought they should see
with their very own eyes.
So they did.
And the friends got a giant surprise!

They saw for themselves
that he wasn't inside.
Still they couldn't believe that he rose,
though they tried.

Floating to Heaven

Later, they hid in a room as before.
They closed all the shutters, they bolted the door.

Then suddenly, Jesus was there in the room,
looking better than when he was laid in the tomb.

Was he really alive? Or was Jesus a ghost?
It seemed to be him. Well, they thought so—almost.

Then he spoke to his friends. He said, "Peace be with you."
And he tried to convince all his friends it was true.

He said, "Why are you troubled, and why do you doubt?
Just look at my hands and my feet. Check 'em out!

"It is I, not a ghost. Is a ghost bones and skin?
See the wound in my side? Take your hand, put it in."

So they did. And at last all his friends really knew—
what the women had said they had seen had been true!

So Jesus hung out with his friends for a while,
till the day that he left with a wave and a smile.

He said, "I must return to my Father above.
You must preach to the world about God's endless love.

"You must preach the good news. You must tell all creation,
and preach of salvation from sin to each nation."

Then he held out his hands, and he lifted them high,
and he blessed all his friends as he rose in the sky.

Up, up Jesus floated, straight up out of sight,
up, up into heaven, to sit at God's right.

His friends all rejoiced as he floated to heaven.
Though Jesus had gone, he had left the eleven.

He'd told them to go and not hide as they'd hid,
and to preach the good news to the world.

So they did.

The Rhyming Bible

How to Draw a Lamb

© HIM Kids 2024

Download These Activity Sheets . . .

The Rhyming Bible

. . . and More at
himkids.com/easterstory.

For Simone and Violet
— Kelly

HIM Kids

The Rhyming Bible Easter Storybook
Text and Illustration Copyright © 2024 by Kelly Pulley

HIM Kids is an imprint of HIM Publications.

Requests for information should be sent via email to HIM Publications. Visit himpublications.com for contact information.

ISBN 978-1-970102-72-7 (Paperback)
ISBN 978-1-970102-73-4 (ePub)
Library of Congress Control Number: 2023948799

Interior design and typesetting: Bryana Anderle (YouPublish.com)
Editor and art direction: Chad Harrington (YouPublish.com)
Theological review: Chad Harrington, MA Biblical Studies, Asbury Theological Seminary
Editorial assistance: Molly Crowson (YouPublish.com)